For my nieces,
Carmen and Nina

Special thanks to Rolf Gates for his inspiration and support
—M.G.

To my family and Dalia
—M.S.

Dial Books for Young Readers
Penguin Young Readers Group • An imprint of Penguin Random House LLC
375 Hudson Street, New York, NY 10014

Printed in China • ISBN 9780399186615 • 10 9 8 7 6 5 4 3 2 1

Design by Jason Henry • Text set in Archer • The artwork for this book was created digitally.

Meditate with Me

A Step-by-Step Mindfulness Journey

Mariam Gates

illustrated by **Margarita Surnaite**

DIAL BOOKS FOR YOUNG READERS

Sit down in a comfortable seat.
Let's start moving from your head to your feet.

Lift your shoulders to your ears.
Flex your arms, and squeeze tight.
Now let it all go, and be loose like spaghetti.

Again—pucker, crinkle, make a face.
Shoulders up, hands clenched, *squeeeeeze*
every part of your body . . . and release.

One more time!
Scrunch everything you can.
Flex your feet, curl each toe.
Take a *deeeeep* breath in,
and then let it go!

Whoosh!

Now notice your breath,
in and out through your nose.
Is the air cool? Is it warm?
Can you feel in your body where it goes?

Place your hand just under your belly button.
Let your next breath fill that spot with air.

Now take your other hand
and place it just above.
Breathe in.
Can you fill that spot too?
Breathe out.

Now bring the bottom hand up
to feel your chest rise and fall.
Fill your chest completely,
and let your spine get tall.

Inhale slowly. . .
     Exhale slowly. . .

Breathe in, and fill your whole body.

Breathe out, and relax your whole body.

Imagine a jar full of water and glitter
in any colors you choose.

Shake this jar a lot.
Keep shaking.
Imagine the colors clouding the water,
zooming this way and that.

When you're ready, stop shaking,
and set the jar down flat.

Wiggle your fingers up high in the air, then bring them slowly toward the ground.
Imagine the glitter floating to the bottom of the jar.
Swish your hands out and down.

Swish!

Your mind is like that glass jar, with shiny thoughts and feelings zooming this way and that.
But you can use your breath and body to set that busy mind down flat.
Gently, just like that. Swish!

You can feel what it's like to be just here, just now.

Breathe in, and fill your whole body.
Breathe out, and relax your whole body.

Your thoughts and feelings
help you in your day.
You need to know when you
are happy or mad or sad.

What does happy feel like in your body?

Make a happy face.
Show happy with your whole body.

What does mad feel like in your body?

Make a mad face.
Show mad with your whole body.

What does sad feel like in your body?

Make a sad face.
Show sad with your whole body.

Now, what does excited feel like in your body?

Make an excited face.
Show excited with your whole body.

Notice your breath again.
Can you fill your whole body like a big balloon?

Breathe in, and fill your whole body.
Breathe out, and relax your whole body.

As you let that breath out slowly,
start to pay attention to the sounds in the room.

Listen.

With your eyes closed and your hands in your lap,
try to hear the sounds all around you,
each bump, beat, and tap.

What do you hear outside?
What do you hear on the street
of your city or town?

Listen.

When you become so quiet,
what else can you hear?

Inside sounds?
Your breathing?
Maybe even your
heart beating?

Breathe in, and fill your whole body.
Breathe out, and relax your whole body.

Listen.

Notice how each sound
comes and then goes.

Notice how each breath
has an easy flow.

Notice how each new thought or feeling has its own rhythm too.
Like clouds in the sky, your thoughts and feelings drift by.
Like glitter in the jar, they move through you.

It's true.

So you can relax, breathe, and listen,
letting everything in and then out today.

Know that this calm place is always just one breath away.

Breathe in, and fill your whole body.
Breathe out, and relax your whole body.

Well done.

Four Easy Steps to Meditate with Me

1 | Sit and Relax

Sit comfortably, and place your hands on your knees or in your lap.

Try squeezing and then relaxing your body to release any tightness (3 times).

Let your spine get tall, and roll your shoulders back.

2 | Breathe and Relax

Bring one hand under your belly button and one hand to your chest.

Try filling each spot with air as if filling a balloon.

Then exhale completely (3 times).

3 | LISTEN AND RELAX

Start to notice the sounds outside the room.

Now try to hear any sounds inside the room.

What do you hear when you are so still and quiet?

4 | RELAX AND BE

Picture a blue sky with white clouds.

Can you be like a big, open sky with clouds drifting by?

Inhale slowly.

Exhale slowly.